AF432251

ACKNOWLEDGMENTS

GRATITUDES

For every shelter that has ever kept me warm and dry.

For every mentor or teacher who has encouraged me to keep going, or helped me to see a new perspective.

For friends and family who have been consistent, caring, and generous with their love and time.

For life lessons that have taught me to value my boundaries, and self-worth, and to believe in myself.

For the gifts of resilience, perseverance, and resourcefulness which were passed down from my ancestors, through my culture, and exemplified in my family.

For meaningful connections and compelling conversations.

For art, music, cinema, games - passions and hobbies which I can genuinely enjoy for hours on end.

For comfort food and moments of serendipity.

For the ever- present opportunity to create and build a life that makes me happy and that I am proud of.

And of course, for my dog, Mia, who has been the best companion a girl could ask for in these trying times - from New York to Edinburgh and beyond.

I am so deeply grateful.

PREFACE

Dear Reader,

Welcome! I hope this collection of poetry and prose finds you well, and if by some chance it hasn't, I hope there's a poem in here that might help, even just a little.

I think we can all agree that these past two years have been "unprecedented", to say the least. Not only has the world had to face drastic changes on an international scale, but individually our livelihoods were each uniquely affected. No two stories, or personal experiences, are alike. Instead, they are all tainted by the same fear of an omnipresent, looming threat.

A Tower of Two Cities is a reflection of my own experiences - a collection of prose and poetry written to process the world through these life-changing events and pieced together in hindsight. For me, this time of transformation was met with an 8- month-long isolation in New York City and then a relocation to Scotland. It felt as if the "ends" and the "beginnings" were all in a constant state of flux, during which time I had to relearn what it meant to be grounded.

Inside, you will find works that celebrate themes of self-expression, personal transformation, social isolation, and growth. You will find that although concepts reflect back on my personal experiences throughout the pandemic, not every poem is in chronological order, some entries were written well before the start of the Covid-19 pandemic, and some are undated. Each entry has the ability to stand wholly on its own, but the order with which the book was curated, the pace, and the tone, are intentional and illustrate an overarching story of a winding trajectory. The hope is that this pattern, this deeper expression of introspection, resilience, self-awareness, and conviction, may be felt when zoomed in but understood when zoomed out.

In tarot, a tower moment is a life-altering time period, where change and transformation affect even our core beliefs pertaining to not only ourselves but the world we exist in. It forces us to look at every aspect of life and determine whether certain relationships, career aspects, or even fundamental beliefs are serving our highest self, or whether they need to be re-evaluated and redefined.

Represented by the tower card, it is often perceived as quite ominous, sometimes met with unease. The imagery itself, being that of a large tower struck by bolts of lightning and crumbling into the fire, is a scene of chaos and utter destruction. The meaning is aligned with a monumental change, endings, and great upheaval. It's easy to see this card as one only indicating negative outcomes, but I believe the deeper meaning of transformation is fundamental and ultimately essential for one's highest good. In other words, growing pains rarely tickle, and recognizing the change as an opportunity to grow, is the key.

I'm putting forward an intention that this collection will find the right people. People who will be able to recognize parts of themselves along this journey. People who will be emboldened and inspired to go after what they desire from this world, and who will finally begin to claim what is rightfully theirs in life. The people who will be encouraged to reflect on their own patterns or who resonate with the idea of deriving meaning from both the light and dark moments, the highs and the lows. I hope this finds the person who feels they are alone in the silence, and that it reminds them that they, indeed, are not.

Even in the face of the unknown, there is something to be gained from the challenge, and in the grand scheme of seasonal growth, you are not alone in the act of facing yours. Though the battle may be long, and at times you will get tired, please know you can (and will) emerge on the other side, better and stronger.

And lastly, though it has been said many times over, in many ways and by many people, it's important to reiterate that - as a collective when we heal and empower ourselves, we heal and empower the world.

With love,
K.

PART I

THE APOCALYPSE

You bask in the dim glow of candlelight.
Shadows flicker across the walls.
Howls and whispers of vacant space, a hollowed emptiness befalls.

With benign fever, and aches of despair.
A crescendo of cacophony was made. An ellipsis of lethal infection
surmounts, this doth render my work day slain.

Day Twelve

Part 1

I think the world might be ending.
All signs point to yes.
Like a memory or a dream, this part's familiar.
Where madness once threatened,
there's happiness instead.
No battle nor tussle. Just a sudden switch.
Skepticism wants to creep but I'm inclined to go with this flow.
Engulfed in love, gratitude, light, and peace - there can be no worse.
Or is this how you know?
Is this another sign? Like the sedating poison of a snake lulling you
into safe slumber before your heart contorts and stops? What's left of
you suddenly laying unravelled before the gods and universe...

Part 2

If the world ended today, would you be okay?

I think I'd go with the flow. Make time for the people I love, go without
pain.

It's true, I've imagined the thrills of breathtaking love, of curing
diseases, and rescuing my family from
generational pains...

But if it all were to end today, I think I'd be content with just enough
time to tell them all I loved them, and that
their light, love, and energy have truly meant the world to me.

Part 3

It's creeping in at the edges, emerging from the recesses.

When the connection stalls, or the picture freezes...
my eyes give a little twitch and my heart starts to quicken.

Someone said the roads are being closed. That to me felt like so much
more than anything else. Beginnings of ends.

All else could be dismissed as hearsay or hysteria but when the roads
finally close and you're trapped inside, staring at blank walls and
streets ran bare, engulfed in sterile silence, how can you stay blind to
the glitches.

Day Fourteen

Hand to heart, rapidly beating -
If I were to perish, I'd want to be honest.
Love is the thing I'd often left unrequited,
The one thing I'd regret if time came too soon.

Not loving deep and not loving true,
To not find soul in the mate of you.
Cursed solitude wins again in the end,
A pushers pull into isolation.

But here lest the words save me some grace,
Love that I've felt in more than one space.

You with the hug to warm the earth,
You with the wit to cure all but one.
You with the knowledge to heal mankind,
You in my dreams who in life I could not find.

And if it is indeed too late,
Breathless words and dreamless fate.
For which foresight all but forsake
Love, purpose, ending worlds.
If indeed it is too late,
Return this dust to heaven's gate -
Of oceans deep and mountains wide,
And the trees that breathe -
 ◊ this borrowed breath I take.

BLACKOUT IN MANHATTAN

August 7, 2020

Blackout in Manhattan
I swear I think I could write,
If it weren't for that piercing silence That high-pitched silence.
There's an emptiness, but it's heavy. It's weighted with the threat of chaotic intent.

She paused. There were sounds of doors slamming off in the distance. Someone else was also awake at 5:15 am. Forceful grunts, aggravated sighs. Same here, she'd thought. It wasn't a particularly rare occurrence for her to be up that late … so late that it became early, but this time she'd actually had a reason. Instead of idly staring at flashes on a screen, lost in someone else's narrative, this time she was creating something, doing something, being someone.

She glanced down to see the life on her phone was dwindling to concerning lows. Barely enough for 2%, but there was no charging it now. She switched on the flashlight, a function she'd rarely used before, other than to find keyholes in the dark after a late night out, but now it seemed vitally important. And yet, even with this newfound necessity, it still managed to be utterly impractical for her to use in this scenario. You see, it's true she needed to see, but she also needed the use of both of her hands, and there was no one around to hold a light for her. In hindsight, a candle probably would've sufficed, it makes no real difference now, but in the small hours of the morning it felt cumbersome and she made do with the tools at hand.

She made her way to the bathroom, propping the phone on the counter, allowing the light to poorly illuminate one wall and part of a mirror. Physics at its best, she thought, and as the light bounced off the glass and illuminated the room with its fractals, she instantly became reminded of her childhood.

The feeling of survival, makeshift, make do. Relics of resourcefulness and pervasive perseverance. Primed by the dark, the scarcity, the anxiety, past realities, and dystopian fantasies propped by lack of sleep. Time seemed to shift as she sat there on the toilet, knowing there would be no internet, no premium, no access…. it dawned on her in the silence.

Without electricity or internet … how could she connect? Genuinely concerned. She was isolated as it was, by this virus that had caused the world to cease and still. Trapped, wasn't a word she would've used before today, it would've felt too dramatic. But, here she was, in a world where as of that day there had been 231,942 total COVID cases and 23,567 total related deaths in New York alone. Talk of the government mobilizing military forces, and terms like "martial law" and "shelter-in-place" were common use … so, yeah, it felt appropriate. Without any virtual way to reach her family who lived out of state, how else could she phrase it? She was alone… and all this time she had been, it had always been just her and her dog. But, at least before help and community were just a phone call away. Now, no one would ever know what happened to her, and she'd never know if they were okay.

She made her way out to the kitchen, absent-mindedly opening the fridge, letting all the cold air out, starving the perishables of their lifeline. Ambulance sirens crescendo outside, along with rampant motor engines of daring opportunists, and other neighbors becoming aware of the blackout in the neighborhood, right here where Tiemann meets Claremont.

There was no telling how long this would continue. Was it intentional? First the pandemic, now the power. How long would survival mode last?

She contemplated packing a bag. At first light, she'd set out on a
journey to Connecticut with her pup in tow. With no car, and no cash
(electronic payment wouldn't be available without the power), she'd
have to procure a bike, or hitch a ride…

And then a whirl of cool air from air conditioning swirled around her,
followed by a
few flickers of light down the hall.

I should really charge my phone.

PART II

UNREST

A Becoming

July 23, 2021

The way time seems to enfold on itself,
The way answers seem to question, "what else?"
The way I compare myself to you comparing to me
The way seasons change, but still remain sky over sea.

Though engagement stones may turn to first homes whilst some are
never wed
Or how love blooms in since empty rooms, where words heard were
never said.
The way some hearts connect for-a-time and some for-ever. The way
some long for days to come which still may never.

And yet still, despite all these, it still seems -

Everyone's becoming something but I'm just wondering what'll become
of me.

A Seeking

May 27, 2021

And even today,
With breath renewed,
You long for something far removed.
To wax and wane-
Restless unease…for nothing quite fulfills the need.
To dot the i's, and cross the t's,
yet, still, conform to marked dis-ease.

In search of all the missing things…
Of life, of soul, of diamond rings.
And even with such efforts keeping—
emptiness resides.
What would it mean if you were seeking —
Something you've hid deep inside.

What if *you* are what you're seeking?

THE GREAT SEA OF DESPAIR

August 14, 2020

I'd been sinking deep into the depths of the Despair, long before I'd realized it was I who'd weighed myself down.
First, it was merely an illusion of sameness, unchanged in every direction. A steady patience resonated within me as I waited for the tides to turn.
They did not.
Weary, I began to dismiss the ever-growing worry that the waters would regret to recede. So some more I waited, blinded by a fervor and the assurance that, "This will get better" and "Soon."
It did not.
The waves did not grow, the sky did not yet darken, and instead, the world remained perfectly still. In the far distances, where sky became the sea, the edge remained unbroken. The still waters stood silent at my supercilious certainty.
Statuesque, I remained and so did she.

Or so I thought,

For, with every passing moment, a small ripple would appear. First around my waist, then my breast and my neck. A small sign, so incremental, that it was incidental to this severity of peril until it was yet, quite literally, beneath my nose.
 And then a thought,
No, an instruction flooded my mind, with great import, one rebuking insanity and ignorance. For with every semblance of same, and conviction of resolution, the only thing that changed was the severity of the predicament. And with great naivety I assumed that a constant obedience could save me, would save me, from this ill- fated doom.
I was wrong.
Utterly and completely so.

Now drowning, unable to swim upward, any hope of breath far out of reach.

The water around me began to bubble, then boil, as the heat of my rage troubled and toiled. And with every turn, every tussle the struggle only became worse. The fight against myself caused me to sink that much further.

So how? How, oh how could I ever hope to survive? When neither submission nor struggle, were the answer to life? Heart racing….

I could not.
There was no third option to this "under" or "over" predicament.
So I stopped.

I stopped struggling and instead observed my surroundings. I observed my heartache and my desire to survive. The limited-ness of the air in my lungs, the captivity of my chest, the lack of breath. The numbness in my fingers and toes. As Despair clawed her way up my feet, pulling me into darkness, I tilted my head up to the sky.
The light trickled in with fractured effort.
Bright as she was, her rays were broken in Despair. I lifted my hands, fingers barely breaking the surface. The heat grazed their tips, and I felt my heart swell. If only I had known, way back in the beginning, to swim before I sank. If only I was strong enough, in the middle, to cast off my despair, and now as I have the light slipping through my fingers if only I could manage to hold on…

I watched as the surface receded, unmoved, unchanged, just as still as before.
My eyes dare not look away. The cold wrapped first around my feet, then my knees, and then my waist. My lungs tightened as the air escaped. And just as I thought I'd be lost forever, disappeared into an abyss, a hand slipped through the surface of the water. Right between the rays, only slightly disrupting the still. If only I deserved it - if I were stronger, smarter, or better. If only I could relinquish my despair and accept your help, then maybe I'd survive… and so yet, despite it all…

That's what I did.

PART III

REBIRTH

Pear(w)l(J)

July 24, 2021

With each foray into a new adventure,
A pattern seems to emerge:
Panic. Excitement. Anxiety. Worry. Fear of Loss. Joy.

Never sequentially, always simultaneously.
Never permanent, but always transcending.
To worry in joy…Or be excited and afraid.
The waves of change, they roll.

A smoothing of coarse, angled sides…
Erosion of walls unknown.
Amounting burns and nerves awry,
From reckless abandon to vertigo —
Such is the rush of the unknown.
Avast, ye stages of change.

Inner Child

When was the last time you looked at your hands through the eyes of your inner child?

Do you remember being transfixed by the translucency of the skin on your inner palms? Vulnerable vessels visible underneath.

Look again, through those eyes. What is it that you see? A change has occurred, and, like you, they've transformed + aged + expanded... but in all this time, had you ever really noticed?

Change is a constant; sometimes occurring swiftly, sometimes at a glacial pace. Look up every now and then and see all that has transpired.

Brilliance

"Do you think Earth ever tires of Sun and Moon?"

Under constant surveillance, their celestial bodies encircling her waiting for her to fail. A body constantly on either side always imposing its power over her form.

"Do you think Earth is in awe of the Sun and Moon?"

Never lonely, always supported by their energetic embrace.

Solar System Series

"What brilliance, what power
Pure cosmic energy.
If only I had half your might
I'd surely be happy
You light the expanse with effortless magic.
You bring warmth to all in need.
If only I could shine as bright
I'd be a better me."
-Earth to Sun

"What grace, and elegance
Calming serenity.
If only I had half your poise
I'd be more worthy.
You illuminate with that heavenly glow.
You glide about with ease.
If only I could dance like you
I'd be a better me."
-Sun to Moon

"What passion, celebration
Joyful reverie.
If only I had half your zeal
I'd be a better me.
You nourish, you shelter
Those that live and breathe.
If only I could sustain life
I'd be less lonely."
-Moon to Earth

Multitudes

July 15, 2020

Yes, I contain multitudes.
Endless layers of complexity
A bundled boundless form
of stories untold.

Skilled to create, to imagine,
To reason, and not just for reckless abandon.
A lifelong mastery in the
elegant art of gauche.
And yet, here I stand
Arms stretched, boots on land.
Overcome, undone.
I'll add, thoroughly transfixed.
For somehow, I've found
Myself lost (entrenched)
In your petals, which length no more than their depth,
And you exist.
You merely exist –
No conditions, no charge, you flourish in tin.

And well,
Quite good, I must think.
What liberty, indeed.
Free to dance, free to be.
Unhindered you are,
by time or perceived reality
And somehow, I think, you just might be
The solution to a question
we're still not quite privy.

Stardust

August 20, 2020

Scattered across all space and time

Unparalleled in your divine

Like lanterns floating 'cross the seas

Or fireflies of woodlands deep

Or stars that shine ever bright

Apart-together on this night.

I'm in awe of your complexity.

Your individual and your entirety.

Elixir

July 24, 2020

He poured the liquid from the vial.
Just enough to top-er up.
Slim shooter, iridescent bile
With lips to lap it up.

"Better just-
all in one,
Else you'll be worse the wear."
Pearled grey and blue
And viscous, too.
He waited, whilst she stared.

What noble cause or great exploit
Could woo such poor decision?
Heartbreak? Yeah.
Failure? Sure.
But clearly, there's no vision.

Big picture lost and at what cost
A life and/or a feeling?
With desperate zeal
To remove all fear
of painful disposition.

If tales were true
No rumored clues
Or blatant signs of mischief.
She might've dared,
A lesser wear, would calm her hearts' contention.

The elixir that she wouldn't shoot
But wished it were the answer,
She tossed it down, high-tailed it out
A win for intuition.

PART IV

CONFLICT

Power

July 23, 2020

What power lies in retrospect.
The power to lift us up and bring us down.
What power lies in our own decision-making, our confidence or lack
thereof.

To be able to say "I've made my mistakes which have paved my road
to now."
What power lies in retrospect?
What power have you found?

The power which resides in our ability to say,
That things will surely happen even if they don't go our way.
The power to confidently own our joys and mistakes
and to therefore say, "well I am what I made."

"And just because I have ownership over past mistakes,
doesn't mean I haven't learned from them", you might say.

We stand tall in knowing that we had shame to bear -
But that we don't let it wither us,
The past has long since disappeared.

So, smile in light of your past failures, heartbreaks, and
misunderstandings.
Smile because the past is NOT the present that you're standing in.

And even now, with heads held high,
past mistakes aren't a reason to hide.
The mistakes of our past have molded us
into who we are today,
So no longer will we cower, no longer are we afraid.

And though you may only remember yourself as someone once
mocked and jeered,
Since we're still remembering, remember to care.
Remember the good times and the laughs,
Remember we're human and not all bad.
Remember love is forever because that was never a lie,
Remember to look past even the darkest of times.

So, when we can remember the good with the bad,
maybe it'll neutralize those feelings that we had.
I'm sorry you were hurt, I hope you forgive the pain you were dealt,
But believe me when I say you are so much more than how you felt.

And as we wander down our separate roads
I bid you the best.
To those left in my journeys past I shall yield the rest:
Don't hate me for whom I used to be so very long ago,
You should know I've grown on past the person you used to know.
I smile, I laugh, I cry, and dance.
I work hard, have goals, and have fun when I can.
I even made more mistakes and learned some lessons new,
but I promise I won't forget the lessons I learned from you.
That's the power of retrospect.

I hope you take great care of yourself and remember that you are deserving of so much more than all you've had to endure.

If harboring hurt and ruminating on pain aren't serving your well-being, consider how you could be kinder to yourself. What tools do you need?

For some, strength exists in the moment after you can acknowledge the past and move on. But for others, strength is decidedly being a safe place for yourself.

Choices

August 5, 2020

One could spend a fortune
And a great deal of time
searching for something they'd never find.
Across the land, deserts, forests, and seas.
Four corners of the earth;
And everywhere in between.

And still,
They'd never find someone that encompasses all that you do.
The sole reason being you're uniquely you.

Not due to a pursuit or future achievement.
Not because you've earned it or won it competing.
Not because you're symmetrical or slightly uneven.
Not for any other reason than just being.

Often misconstrued for a destination,
The "path to happiness" is not a race we take place in.
Your happiness is determined by your internal value,
Your connections, your fulfillment,
Your enjoyments and outlooks.
So, no need to feel guilty, ashamed, or afraid.
You deserve to be happy...right now, today.

Turbulence

We pass through the clouds, majestic and enchanting and it is without fear we allow ourselves to become engulfed; we have thusly succumbed.

Like feathers atop the air we breathe, we give into the light majesty that is uncertainty and curiosity.

I waited, eyes wide as we divulged, the last bit of sun-kissed sky lingering, illuminating the wafting peaks. Perpetual longing and spirit yearning as we descended into the superfluous wafts of unparalleled pristine.

We engaged, stomachs dropping, yells of disconcerting fear; Our minds focused on the destination and the guidance. Flashes of light, pillars, and bolts narrow us into a deeper, darker depth.
Eyes closed, but only briefly as a newly changing environment quickly approaches and the heavenly, cerebral existentialism slowly dissipates.

Calm quiet, as the tumultuous turbulence gives way to the darkness below. What was once as kind as a pillow has morphed, harsh and raw, into monster-villain-evil. Dark skies linger beneath.

What revelations? What postulations and highfalutin profundity have you to cast now? Has some awareness been prolonged? Or is your newfound perception and enlightenment merely feigned exuberance and cheap wine?

Earth rises, dirt manifests.

PART V

PERSEVERANCE

Resurrection

October 5, 2021

The me you know has died,
Slain by sword and fire.
Build upon thy ash and bones
With lives anew entirely.

The me you know ceases,
Gone with wind and rain.
The earth and sky collapsed behind
For nothing gold can stay.

The me you know has vanished,
And with her all that's sane.
With stranger's eyes, her heart still cries
For you, she mourns in vain.

SETTLED

September 24, 2021
Edited: July 5, 2022
Morningside, Edinburgh

There are times I feel wholly miserable.
Displaced, redundant.
Riddle with fears of "what if".

Sometimes I fear that I overshare just to get this weight off of my chest and then I instantly regret the vulnerability.

[But if I may, for a moment over-indulge, perhaps just for myself - but maybe also for anyone else … any "strong", "independent" individual … who might feel seen in this moment.]

I worry that I overshare these thoughts -
Thoughts of crying late hours of the night, complaining about social anxiety, and panic attacks. It's embarrassing, mostly because I'd been so vocal about how great of a decision I was making in the first place. But here I am, all of those things, wondering if I've made a mistake.
I want so desperately to wake up and feel in place. Settled.
But I'm starting to realize that may never happen. Most likely will never happen. It won't ever happen. [she wrote, unknowingly.]

No matter what I'm looking for – no matter what "fit" or "belong" means to me, I'll never find the exact environment, or experience the correct sequence of events to convince me.

No preconceived notion I have about belonging will apply to any scenario here because the setting, the medium for the experiment, is unlike any I'd ever been in before and as a result the entire basis of my calculations is incorrect.

How do I account for a confounding variable such as location or culture, when I truly just don't know what I don't know? [How could I disregard the possibility of the inverse? Where additional variables may come in and require a new and different equation.]

How do I relate to others from my perspective of wildly flailing and searching, when their perspective is so displaced from my own? [Why do I assume everyone else has it all figured out? When it's obvious they don't.]

Every attempt to relate or understand becomes contorted as cliché or self-centered. I'm just trying to consume your world in small, relatable bites. Trying to draw parallels to the world I knew, even such a world as it was, with its own insurmountable levels of unknown.

What I'm trying to say is that I have never been more convinced that I don't know anything. I am but a small speck of overlapping experience – an eye with a lens of contorted view. Black, female, child of immigrants – from a nation that hates her and that makes mistakes on an international scale – now a spotlight, an association, a magnet for the bias that comes from the distillation of such a place, and such a history.

I am – anxious, and hyper-self-aware. I am my own worst critic. I am aching to be free and loved and accepted and desired and settled.

I am longing for a home.

A Remembrance of Self

August 20th, 2014

And I refuse to be your muse.

Something new to light the fuse, ignite the rights and the wrong, and

defy your petty song.

I refuse to jump and dance,

be a jester while you pass all your judgment

on what I represent.

I refuse to be a novelty, something new for you to try. An excuse, an

experiment, an inhumane lie.

I refuse to stand and watch while you tear it all apart - what we've built

with our hands and carried in our hearts,

that which you manipulate with your thoughts.

I refuse to be a means for your gain and yours alone.

PART VI

RESILIENCE

TRAVELLER

January 2, 2022
Morningside, Edinburgh

It's taken me a moment but I've come to a realization. The 'me', that is
I, is not the 'me' that you see.
Everyone's lives are comprised of their own experiences – what they
see, what they read, what they choose to believe. What they're told and
the internalized flecks of all intangible things. We create worlds and
ideas and torture ourselves with them, but we also project them onto
others. We expect and assume – based on our lived experiences
(whether absolute or skewed is up for debate), we believe these things
to be true (self-evident). And as we all reside somewhere along the
spectrum of Self-Awareness … sometimes at different points, and
different times … it's impossible to say that any one of us has lived a
life without the mistake of misjudgment.

That being said (with all benefits of doubt exhausted)….I have learned
that I am not what you think you know. I exist in my own independent
universe, though I have traversed many others. Whether as a visitor for
a moment or for a while, I've at some point found myself in someone
else's orbit. They haven't always been the most welcome of
experiences.

In the past, I convinced myself that in order to exist I had to contend
with the projections of whom others may have thought I was. It caused
me to hurt, feel uncomfortable, and question my self-worth. There
were times when I thought I'd never measure up to their ideas of
perfect, or that I'd crumble under the weight of assumption. But it is
only recently, as I've made the largest leaps outside of my own comfort
zone, that I've been able to see – I am entirely removed from your
mind's eye of me.

47

You see… I am me, and I've grown and learned along the way that the spirit of me does not change. And with each dip into each new culture or "universe", I carry with me that sameness… and now also a revelation.

It is you that changes. The figurative "you", which exists outside of me. With each foray into a new universe comes new challenges, requirements, expectations, and assumptions.

Who I shouldn't be, what I shouldn't do, how I should talk/act/dress … how I should exist. But, I've learned that I no longer need to shape-shift. I don't need to assign importance to these walls of confinement. Don't get me wrong, I'll learn the waves of your waters, but only so that I may communicate how expansive my soul is. I'll comprehend what you deem to be the laws of reality, but only so that the light of my spirit may also ignite the light of your own. Maybe then, once you've become more open, can we build something beautiful together. Until then, please know, you are not entitled to my essence nor my entirety.

That's reserved for me, and me alone.

Affirmations

I give myself permission to rest and take breaks when necessary.

I am allowing myself to take up as much space as I need, when I need it, without fear of being too much.

I allow myself to ask for and be receptive to help when I need it.

I advocate for myself because my wants, needs, safety, and interests are all valid.

I am deserving of love and kindness.

I am enough.

Would You Rather?

If you were told you could have everything you desired (things which you didn't already possess) but it would cost you one thing you already have and love, would you accept?

If the cost of achieving your dreams was the lesson of letting go of old comforts and habits that no longer served you,
would you take the risk?

Or would you rather stay uncomfortable in your comfort zone?

Would you rather stay where you are out of fear of the unknown, fear of loneliness and heartbreak, fear of not knowing if you have what it takes?

Or would you rather... *insert risky dreams here*

DREAMER

January 31, 2022
Morningside, Edinburgh

This is for the creative kids with the big hearts and wild imaginations. For the inner child, that dreamed of bright skies, wicked adventures, and pure adulation. This is for you and me, and them and some others. This is for the kid who wished more would come, but grew tired and couldn't recover. For the deep heart who internalized a happiness out of reach, someone who dreamed of picket fences or adoring fans and money. Someone who wanted their entire life transformed at the drop of a pin, the longing in their heart growing like a heavy conventional waiting.

Days and nights pass before your eyes, and you wonder why it worsens. You hope, you pray, you're confused by the delays. The obstacles, the detours. The accidents... Surely, these all mean you're not meant to have anything. You're not meant for joy, love, or beauty. You're not meant to own what others discard so freely. You're not meant for anything and that must be your fault entirely. Not priceless, but worthless and a waste of breath and earth....

Well, this is the hard part, my dear Soul. The part we dread and hate, the unlearning and revealing of things we can't quite shake. This longing you have has seemed to take hold. It has caused an obscurity of brightness in your soul.

But what if I said - all you knew was false.

The flashy, the bling, and the elation are wrong. Not to be disheartening, or unbearably bleak – but to free you of the mental stronghold which enslaves your spiritual needs. Your need for connection, purpose, peace, and light. Your need to heal the inner you, so you can soar in your own right.

Not along flight plans outlined in manufactured dreams – but based on the singing and warmth, you experience down deep.

What if I told you that to thrive you have to fail, and only once you learn to flail in the unknown, then will you begin to really set sail, to succeed on your trail. Your own personal trajectory which would be unlike any other's is an epic tale that forces you to fight many monsters. To learn from mistakes, over and over and over again.
A test of your faith, your ability, your intuition. A winding path that has its highs and lows, but a worthy one throughout which your spirit grows.

It is not easy. It's not all dancing on the beach at sunset or champagne on rooftops. But the ability to preserve is necessary for a shot at sustainable happiness. So make your choice, that's how it starts – live for yourself or you stay in the dark. Live for you or die in the dark?

February 24, 2022

Today I've been thinking about how we are not only the best parts of ourselves but also the worst parts. The light and dark, the inhale and exhale. There is a balance in being able to acknowledge and accept the ups and downs, and know that we're deserving of love in our entirety.

I am here

I found myself in solitude again.
But this time I found myself -
When I learned to embrace the silence
When I accepted the good with the bad
When I learned to respond instead of react
When I became selective with my energy
And when I became intentional with where I placed my attention.

I had to uncover whether it was nature or nurture which drove me to desire connection in the way that I did - longing, needing, more than just a desire but a want disguising a lack Recognizing the duality of being both scared of rejection and also scared of being seen because to me

seeing me -> is knowing me -> is loving me

and if someone can leave (and forget) after all of that, then what did that say about me?

Learning that I am not defined by the actions of others but by the character of my soul and that people often operate from a perspective that is entirely their own (informed by their own internal universes) ... and understanding that the love I've experienced is due in part to the love that I've shared and when harnessed that knowledge ... that love ... is power and freedom.

I used to pride myself on hyper-independence
I used to equate loneliness with self-worth
I used to fear that if I took up too much space, I'd push everyone away.
I used to think that all I had to offer was just how neatly I could fit into the world or how much I could achieve.

I used to.
But not anymore -
Now I'm choosing to live life on my own terms.

I am choosing to rest when I want, create when I want, and take up as much space as I need.
I am choosing to take that extra deep breath or pause in silence and solitude when I need to return to myself in the chaos.

I am choosing to trust my intuition and honor it when I know that something is just not right for me.
I am choosing to color outside of all lines and honor my own self-motivated achievements.

And in all of this, I validate myself fully.

EPILOGUE

March 3, 2022

Sunshine and Rain

Some days are a dream
Colors are bright, the air is sweet and I'm floating through the peace and bliss I've cultivated.

Other days are harder. More work, less romance.

The real skill is learning to appreciate both equally. To not get too attached or fixated on either. To understand everything is temporary, and that it's all a balance.

I'm still learning to enjoy the sunshine with the rain.

I hope you are too.

Lessons Learned

July 5th, 2022

Dear Reader,

Thank you for coming on this journey with me! I never thought I'd be sharing these pieces of myself with anyone, so thank you for being a part of this. It's been quite a liberating experience, being able to take all of the emotions and thoughts that have been accumulating over these past few years and lay them down, connecting things in hindsight that I wasn't able to back then.

I hope that you felt connected, in some way, to these works. Whether that be feeling immersed in the writing, or being able to relate to concepts of personal growth, perseverance, or self-appreciation. I think one thing we can all agree on is that these past few years have been incredibly challenging, and isolation has forced us to acknowledge even the most hidden aspects of ourselves.

I know many of us have undergone personal transformations, and will continue to do so many times over - and there's always that lingering anxiety of "what next?"… but I hope that reflecting in this way, along with me, reminded you of the strength and courage we each possess.

I shared my draft of this collection with a dear friend of mine, and her response was so encouraging I just needed to share it with you all.

She said, "It's easy to get lost in the bleakness and uncertainty of the world [especially with Covid]. But, even with so much changing in your surroundings, it's important to understand the changes and greatness within yourself and acknowledge it and not lose sight of yourself."

I hope we never forget how in even the darkest of moments, we united globally - showing empathy for strangers, celebrating the outstanding efforts of emergency responders, health care workers and teachers. We chose to remember what it means to recognize humanity in one another, and fight for our core rights – I hope we never lose sight of that.

I hope that the lessons we were forced to learn in the ebbs can be fruitful to ourselves and beneficial to others, whilst we're in our flows. I hope you never lose sight of yourself. <3

Sincerely,
K.

P.S. If you've enjoyed this, and found some connection or meaning - whether from a line or a stanza - I'd love to hear from you, it would mean so much!